Original title:
Terrariums and Time

Copyright © 2025 Creative Arts Management OÜ
All rights reserved.

Author: Finn Donovan
ISBN HARDBACK: 978-1-80581-924-0
ISBN PAPERBACK: 978-1-80581-451-1
ISBN EBOOK: 978-1-80581-924-0

Enclosed Worlds Whispers

Inside a glass, a kingdom spins,
Tiny creatures, let the fun begin!
They throw a party, no room to roam,
Each leaf a dance floor, their little home.

The cactus jokes about its prickly fate,
While the fern sways, saying it's never late.
They sip on dew, a treetop toast,
Cheering on the snail, the party host!

Memories Suspended in Spheres

In a bubble floats a hamster wheel,
It dreams of cheese, oh what a meal!
The memories bubble, then pop with glee,
As a wise old turtle hums by the pea.

Goldfish plot their next grand escape,
Wishing for legs, a whole new shape!
A lizard laughs, it can't help but smirk,
As they swirl in this whimsical work.

Microcosms of Forgotten Minutes

In a nook of glass, a realm so small,
A gnat plays chess, though it can't recall.
With crumbs for pawns, they strategize,
Each move a chuckle, oh what a surprise!

The snails debate their favorite shade,
While ants march on, plans well-laid.
Minutes are muddled, lost in the fun,
While dandelion clocks tick, one by one.

Nature's Secrets in a Sealed Haven

A clever squirrel hides its stash,
Amongst the plants, it makes a dash.
Earthworms giggle, dressed in dirt,
Throwing confetti, they pull their shirt.

The ladybug lends her little tune,
As friends slide in, like they're on a cartoon.
Beneath glass roofs, the antics begin,
In a cozy world where all can win!

Enclosed Echoes of Eternity

In glassy halls, the lizards plot,
A dance of dust, they jiggle a lot.
Moss whispers tales of a distant snack,
While tiny frogs give a ribbiting whack.

The snails wear homes that shine like gold,
While crickets chirp secrets of old.
All sit still in a leafy lounge,
As time ticks softly, a cheeky sound.

Timeworn Sprouts in a Sealed Realm

A leafy world where shadows play,
Plants wear hats in a quirky way.
The roots engage in whispered chats,
While bugs debate on top of mats.

In this dome where the light is odd,
A flower laughs, "Look, I'm a god!"
But petals droop at the silliest sight,
As laughter echoes into the night.

Fragments of Earth Frozen in Glass

Beneath the dome, the moments freeze,
A ladybug sneezes, oh what a tease!
Pebbles gossip, the crickets sigh,
As the stars in jars wave the night goodbye.

A cactus winks, "I'm the king of cool,"
While thrifty ferns plot to rule the school.
In this miniature land where quirks abound,
Who knew such fun could be found?

Lush Landscapes in a Captive Dome

Inside this dome, where oddities thrive,
The beetles dance, as if they're alive.
Ferns try their hand at a stand-up show,
While wiggles of worms steal the spotlight glow.

Here laughter builds like the moss on ground,
With secrets of soil that are never found.
In a world where the wild and the silly collide,
Each moment captured, a curiosity ride.

The Stillness of Nature's Clock

In a jar, the world sits tight,
A tiny, lush, and funny sight.
Frogs play chess with flies and bees,
While time stands still among the leaves.

The snail's a champion, slow and sly,
With a trophy shell, oh my, oh my!
Minutes drip like honey sweet,
As ants groove to their tiny beat.

Secrets Beneath the Leafy Canopy

Beneath the greens, a party brews,
With dancing bugs in tiny shoes.
A worm recites his best joke yet,
While crickets hum—a band, you bet!

The ferns all nod, the mosses cheer,
For laughter shared is worth a year.
In this lushness, secrets hide,
From shrooms to roots, they dance with pride.

Moments Stilled in Glassy Spaces

Inside the glass, a world confined,
Where time's a friend that's hard to find.
The beetles race in tiny cars,
Chasing after dreams of stars.

A tiny dragon with a crown,
Is king of all that mossy town.
With laughter echoing through the air,
These moments pause, but no one cares.

A Universe Encapsulated

In a bubble of green delight,
A universe that feels just right.
The sunbeams tickle leaves so bright,
While time giggles, drifting light.

A jolly lizard, wearing specs,
Counts each ant and all their checks.
With every tick, a gnome will cheer,
In this realm, there's naught to fear.

Once Upon a Leaf

A leaf once dreamed of flying high,
But stuck in glass, it sighed and cried.
With roots beneath, it wiggled slow,
'This is my stage, not the skies' show!'

The bugs would gossip day and night,
'Why does it grow with all its might?'
'It's plotting escape, or so they say,
But here it is, happy to stay!'

Vignettes of Growth within Boundaries

In soil confined, the sprouts would cheer,
'Look at us dance, we have no fear!'
The sunlight beams from a tiny hole,
Tickling leaves, making them roll.

They threw a party, oh what a sight,
With moss for music, all felt light.
A worm brought snacks, all juicy and sweet,
While tiniest raindrops played their beat.

Reflections in a Crystal Sphere

Inside a globe, a world unfolds,
Tiny tales of green are told.
'Look at my roots!' a sprout would boast,
'While you just float, I'm the thriving host!'

The glass is fogged, yet smiles abound,
As miniature creatures dance around.
'A jungle feast!' cried tiny moss,
In these small spaces, we're the boss!

The Silence of Growing Things

In a bubble, plants keep quiet games,
Whispering secrets with funny names.
'Why grow so tall when short is chic?'
A fern mused soft, 'Let's not be sleek!'

They played hide and seek under the light,
'The sun's our tagger; we must be light!'
Laughter erupted, though none could hear,
In their own world, they had no fear.

Reveries in Glassy Strip

In a jar snug and round,
A tiny world is found.
Mice dance on top of grass,
While the plants stare and pass.

A squirrel rides a snail,
In its shell, it sets sail.
Laughter fills the air,
Who knew they'd make such a pair?

Frogs throw a picnic feast,
In a leaf, they host the beast.
Cake made of dewdrop sweet,
With ants serving a treat.

The sun gives a cheeky grin,
While shadows play a spin.
Time giggles, takes a break,
In this glass, a silly lake.

Secrets of Seasons in Suspended States

In glassy halls of fame,
Where leaf and bud play game.
A snowman sips his tea,
While bees hum merrily.

The autumn's laugh hides near,
With pumpkin pie and cheer.
Winter shivers with a frown,
In cozy mossy gown.

Each change whispers, 'Look at me!'
In a sway of jubilee.
Frogs wear scarves, oh so bright,
While sit in daydreams of night.

Sunbeams tease with a wink,
As marbles spin and clink.
In this jar, seasons twirl,
Dance their funny little whirl.

A Timeless Tale in Lush Greenery

In a jungle of delight,
Time tickles, quite the sight.
Lizards playing tag with bees,
While whispering through the trees.

A snail writes tales on leaves,
Of brave bugs and buzzing thieves.
Reflecting on a drip,
That holds a thousand trip.

The grasses giggle low,
As shadows start to glow.
A dance-off with the breeze,
Spinning dreams with such ease.

Past meets future in a loop,
As critters create a troop.
In this green, where time's a friend,
The laughter never ends.

Diminutive Dreams of Life

In jars of glass, the critters prance,
Tiny tales in a leafy dance.
With every tick, their laughter grows,
As they plot where today's adventure goes.

A snail in shades, pursuing speed,
While crickets sing the garden's creed.
In this small realm, no cares to find,
Just whimsical tales of the quirky kind.

The earthworms watch, they raise a brow,
As the beetles argue who's right - or wow!
The sun may set on a giant stone,
But here, they groove like they own the throne.

With winks and giggles, these critters thrive,
Lived in a jar, yet oh so alive!
In playful worlds where laughter sings,
Life's pint-sized stage has endless springs.

The Gardens That Hold Infinity

Beneath a dome of glassy hues,
A potted realm where whimsy brews.
Each leaf a story, each stone a prank,
The tiny mice debate their rank.

A quirky frog with a tiny crown,
Rules the space like a jester in town.
The ants all giggle; the worms applaud,
As cucumber vines are slightly flawed.

Time's a joker in this playful land,
Where days and nights dance hand in hand.
With playful blooms in colorful rows,
The gnomes trade secrets no one knows.

Oh, what a world wrapped tight in glass!
Where moments bend, and giggles pass.
In gardens bright, where laughter's free,
Life is a jest, come laugh with me!

Verdant Memories in Transparent Shells

In bubbles green, where whimsy plays,
Frogs wear hats on sunny days.
A cactus sings to a curious beetle,
While secrets grow like a whisper's needle.

The soil grins as roots entwine,
As snails pursue their race divine.
Each droplet drips with tales so silly,
As bushes sway, oh what a frilly!

With petals bright and ferny cheer,
The daffodils wish the pigeons near.
In this square world, so snug and neat,
Giggles sprout from each tiny seat.

As memories swell in jars so wide,
The creatures laugh through the moonlit slide.
In fanciful realms of green delight,
Lies mischief's dance, both bright and light.

Green Worlds Spinning Slowly

In glassy orbs, the moments spin,
With toads in tuxedos, where to begin?
The ferns all whisper sneaky dreams,
While ladybugs laugh in silly schemes.

A flower twirls in a breezy jig,
While crickets play a tiny gig.
The shadows stretch and giggles share,
As roots embrace without a care.

A bouncy gnome trips over a stone,
Cackles rise, but he won't moan.
For in this reel of verdant cheer,
Every misstep draws a laugh near.

As time takes dance on a green-lit stage,
Life's quirks and quirks turn the page.
With every laugh and every grin,
These worlds spin slowly, where joys begin.

When Clocks Slow Down

When my plants start to ponder,
Do they need a watch or maybe a wand?
They stretch and yawn in the light,
As seconds giggle and scurry beyond.

With their leaves all a-wobble,
And soil like a soft, mossy bed,
They whisper secrets to the sun,
While I just sip tea and scratch my head.

Oh, the days they dance and twirl,
As I chase my cat through the lounge,
The clock's hands stuck in a swirl,
While my green friends playfully lounge.

In this leafy escape of cheer,
Where the seconds seem to dissolve,
I laugh at my clock's sneaky ways,
As nature takes charge and resolves.

Resilience Blooming Under Glass

Behind this glassy dome of green,
The world outside is wild and loud,
Yet here, it's calm, serene—
Like introverts in a crowd.

Little buds giggle in glee,
As the sun plays tag with the shade,
Each sprout holds a tiny decree,
Of resilience wildly displayed.

The rain pitter-patters a song,
While the soil hums a soft tune,
Here, nothing feels wrong or long,
As life blooms to the rhythm of noon.

With a chuckle and a sway,
Each leaf learns to flutter and jive,
In their cozy glassy ballet,
They teach me, once more, how to thrive.

Pocketed Wilderness and Histories

In my tiny glass park, true gems thrive,
With histories etched in their veins,
They giggle as they strive,
Telling tales of sunshine and rains.

Each leaf a memoir, a tiny scroll,
Whispering secrets of years gone by,
While I fumble for a bowl,
To catch the chunks of dust that fly.

Nature tucked in a little nook,
Mocking the speed of life's race,
As I pause and take a look,
At the humor of this green space.

So here's to the wild in a box,
With roots that dance and twine,
They laugh at watches and clocks,
And make every second divine.

The Space Between Growth and Time

In the gap where moments stretch,
And seedlings push towards the stars,
They chase after dreams they sketch,
While avoiding the buzz of cars.

With calendars tossed out the door,
And sunlight pouring in like wine,
They put on a show on the floor,
Growing wild, like an unplanned design.

Each sprout a prankster in disguise,
Every glance holds a cheeky grin,
As they play tag with the skies,
While I wonder where the day's been.

It's a game of tick-tock surprise,
Where growth holds the lead and the sway,
While I chuckle at life's silly ties,
In this little patch where I play.

Tiny Ecosystems of Yesterday and Tomorrow

In a glass jar, wonders dwell,
A leafy kingdom, can you tell?
Tiny critters dance and sway,
Pretending it's a sunny day.

Mossy hills and twigs so fine,
Each little creature sipping brine.
They plot and plan with such a glee,
While we humans sip our tea.

Giant leaves hide secrets bold,
Stories of the young and old.
While we rush, they take their ease,
Time for them just bends and frees.

So here's to worlds in glass confined,
Where laughter echoes, intertwined.
With nature's whimsy, life's a show,
In little realms where time runs slow.

The Passages Within a Captured Globe

Inside this dome of crystal clear,
Lies a forest full of cheer.
Fungi giggle, mosses sigh,
As if they'd tell the moon goodbye.

A beetle dons a tiny hat,
While snails ride on their backs, how fat!
Time winks as a leaf falls down,
And wonders who will wear the crown.

Sunbeams push against the glass,
Bouncing light, oh what a class!
While we squint with puzzled brows,
In their world, they take a bow.

So watch them march in their parade,
In a tiny realm, laughter's made.
Here, the hours flutter about,
As they joke and play, no doubt.

Nature's Clockwork in Silicate

In a dome where shadows play,
Nature's gears spin day by day.
A ladybug readies for a race,
While the dirt just finds its place.

Between the roots, a party brews,
With sparkling drops and morning blues.
Tick-tock goes the sly old tree,
Winking slyly, can't you see?

Time may pause for us outside,
But here, it's a vibrant ride.
With every tick, the critters cheer,
Creating moments we hold dear.

So laugh with them in this little dome,
Where every creature calls it home.
Inside this clock, the hours play,
Creating joy in every way.

Capsules of Change

In glassy shells where wonders dance,
Life takes a turn, a merry chance.
Bacteria throw a kooky bash,
While ferns just wiggle in a flash.

A roly-poly takes a spin,
In a world both tall and thin.
Each pebble holds a tiny tale,
As winds blow in a playful gale.

Here in pockets of contained mirth,
Life's growth shows just what it's worth.
With every bloom, a wink, a jest,
In these capsules, nature's best.

So raise a toast to the wiggly crew,
In vibrant shades of green and blue.
Within these orbs, the future gleams,
Crafting merriment with all its themes.

Hourglass Gardens

In a jar, the plants take root,
They laugh as we chase our loot.
Tiny worlds, so much to see,
All without a trip to the sea.

Time ticks by, or does it stall?
These greens have no cares at all.
We water them with our best plans,
Yet they grow better than our fans.

Sprinkling soil like fairy dust,
In our whims, we place our trust.
Each angle offers a new surprise,
Like a prank played by garden spies.

So here we stand, in sparks of mirth,
As they plot to take over the Earth.
With each bloom, they silently chime,
"Why don't we just forget about time?"

Memories in Miniature

A miniature world trapped in glass,
Where memories grow and brightly pass.
A tiny tree, and things that roam,
In this little house, they make their home.

They giggle as we fumble about,
Trying to remember what it's all about.
Each sprout whispers old jokes in glee,
While we search for the truth, like a lost key.

Raise a toast to our botanical friends,
With their shenanigans that never ends.
Forget your troubles, everything's fine,
In their small kingdom, we sip our wine.

Every layer tells stories anew,
Of forgotten moments and skies so blue.
In this glass realm, laughter swells,
As crazy green tales each bubble tells.

Sanctuary in a Jar

A smile shines from soil so deep,
Where no worries disturb their sleep.
A sanctuary for all things spry,
Beneath a lid as clouds float by.

They snicker as we peek inside,
In our world, they're off to ride.
With moss for mountains and rocks for hills,
Watch as they raise their tiny thrills.

Whimsical roots that dance and sway,
To a beat no human can play.
They plot their escape with every inch,
While we only glance and give a pinch.

Locked away, they jest and tease,
No deadlines here, only the breeze.
Rich green laughter, a carnival scene,
In a jar, where we all can lean.

Lush Echoes of Yesterday

In a vessel, a riot of green,
Whispers of the long, unseen.
Leafy echoes of days gone by,
Ticklish secrets where shadows lie.

They chuckle at our mundane strife,
In their small world, they cherish life.
Each flicker of light sparks a grin,
Who knew that joy could dwell within?

We plant our dreams in soil so neat,
While they dance in their leafy suite.
Tiny worlds waltzing on each shelf,
Sowing laughter, growing themselves.

So here's to the jests of the sprout,
In every leaf, a giggling shout.
As we rush on, they simply smile,
In their lush realm, they stay awhile.

Blindfolded Gardens in Temporal Containers

In a jar full of dirt, I planted my dreams,
But they sprouted with feet and began to scheme.
They danced on the shelf, wearing hats made of grass,
While I stood there, chuckling, letting time pass.

Each leaf held a secret, a joke in the shade,
A cactus told tales that were slightly frayed.
With soil for a stage, they performed quite a show,
Blindfolded, I laughed as my plants stole the glow.

Beneath glassy ceilings, their antics were grand,
They whispered of journeys to a far off land.
In a world tucked away, they'd fumble and trip,
While I just enjoyed my front-row seat trip.

Oh, the fun in this glass, where chaos is planned,
Where a fern plays the lead with a sprout as a brand.
I'll celebrate life in this tiny bazaar,
Where humor and dirt keep my spirits ajar.

The Essence of Growth in an Hourglass

With grains of a moment, I planted a seed,
In an hourglass realm, it grew quite a breed.
The roots grasped for time, while the leaves took a bow,
A rapid little dance, oh, what a show now!

As seconds slipped through, my plant made a face,
Sticking out tiny limbs, invading my space.
Beneath the watchful glass, it plotted and played,
While I, sipping tea, just let it cascade.

I think it is winning the race of our days,
With each tiny root stretching in funny ways.
It giggled and wriggled, then took off its hat,
Claiming all the time while I just sat and sat.

In a flip of the sand, my humor would grow,
As my leafy companion stole all of the show.
So here is the truth: in this glass, so sly,
We both laugh at moments darting by, oh my!

Chronicles of the Enclosed Expanse

In a box full of green, where mystery flows,
My plants held court with stories nobody knows.
With twigs as their wands, they conjured missed dreams,
Each bubble a saga, or so it seems.

They shared witty tales of a snail's brief dash,
And laughed at the shadows that danced with a splash.
In whispers so soft, they spoke of delight,
While I just sipped cocoa, enjoying the night.

To the outside world, it's just dirt on a shelf,
But inside their realm, they are quite the elf.
With secrets and laughter in a chamber so small,
I'm just the audience, enthralled by it all.

In this whimsical world, they're kings and I'm fool,
Every pebble and leaf is a mischievous tool.
So come take a look, at this glassy expanse,
And share in the fun of a plant's silly dance.

A Mosaic of Life Captured

Enclosed in clear walls, a colorful scene,
A patchwork of chaos, a jungle so keen.
The pebbles were gossiping under the sun,
While leaves giggled softly, all having their fun.

Each plant had a quirk, a trait quite absurd,
With a vine that could jiggle, or branches that stirred.
In this tiny collage, time took a few bows,
As my roots made friends with a pot of spry brows.

With moments locked up, the hilarity brewed,
As sprouts flipped their hair, in a frenzy, they grew.
The mint teased the basil, "I'm better with pies!"
While the poor little thyme just sighed soft goodbyes.

So here's to the laughs in this glassy retreat,
Where fibers of life make for quite the beat.
In the dance of the leaves, the humor's alive,
A mosaic of silliness in which we thrive.

Growth in Quiet Spaces

In glassy homes, the secrets thrive,
Where tiny worlds begin to jive,
A leaf says, "Hey, I need some sun!"
While dust bunnies claim it's all just fun.

Mossy cushions, a cozy bed,
Little critters dance and tread,
In silence, they plot their leafy schemes,
While humans snooze, lost in dreams.

A sip of water, a sprinkle here,
Whispers of life that we may not hear,
They think they're kings, with roots and grit,
Let's grab some snacks, and enjoy their wit.

Yet in this jar, we've made a mess,
With soil and joy, we're all compressed,
Who knew that growth could be so neat?
In silly spaces, the world's a treat.

Preserved Paradises

Inside a dome, where laughter breathes,
A jungle's soul with tiny leaves,
A squirrel once tried to take a peek,
And left behind a nut to squeak.

The cacti giggle, the ferns are proud,
In micro jungles, they stand loud,
A dance of petals, a humorous brawl,
As if the plants are having a ball.

Each little sprout has quirky dreams,
Plotting their paths with giggles and gleams,
A terracotta turtle stole the scene,
Claiming he's the garden's queen.

In jars of glass where fun can grow,
The worlds collide, yet slow and low,
With smiles aplenty, come peek inside,
For in their silence, they take pride.

A Symphony of Stillness

In a glass stage, the actors play,
With roots and stems in grand ballet,
A thimble of water, a rickety chair,
Their silent laughter fills the air.

Mushrooms whisper, "You're looking great!"
While tiny bugs debate their fate,
They wiggle and giggle, oh what a sight,
In their lilypad hats, they're feeling bright.

The world outside rushes, fast and loud,
While in this bubble, they form a crowd,
A starry night made of mossy dreams,
Where the sunlight bursts and brightly beams.

So let us pause, take in the show,
Where silence speaks, and laughter flows,
For in their realm of green and blue,
The jokes are fresh, and friendships true.

The Garden Within

Beneath the lid, where whimsy dwells,
A garden grows with giggles and spells,
The tiny plants, like jesters, frolic,
In this sandy realm, they're quite symbolic.

With pebbles tuned to a chime's light,
And twigs proclaiming it's "Tumbleweed Night,"
The sunshine winks from a glassy dome,
While ants gossip about their home.

Every sprout has a tale to tell,
Of adventures grand, and mischief that fell,
With roots intertwined in a dance so sweet,
They hold their breath until we meet.

So tiptoe softly, don't startle a leaf,
For they'll spill secrets, beyond belief,
In gardens within, laughs intertwine,
With joy and growth—oh, how divine!

The Slow Dance of Roots

In a jar where ferns do sway,
The roots are having their ballet.
Wiggling round without a care,
Tap-tap-tapping, a soil affair.

Tiny dancers in brown shoes,
Doing twists with mossy views.
They've got moves that laugh and spin,
A funky party deep within.

With each layer, a new surprise,
A beetle joins, much to our eyes.
With smiles wide and pebbles bright,
They groove through day and into night.

So grab a glass and peek inside,
Where roots and laughter do abide.
A waltz of whimsy, oh so neat,
In this little world, we can't be beat!

Green Dreams in Glass

Within a glass, the greens conspire,
They dream up plans that never tire.
A sprout shouts, "I'll grow so tall!"
While cacti just roly-poly, fall.

A mossy mound, a comfy bed,
For bugs that nod off, dreams in their head.
"Just don't forget," the parsley winks,
"To wake us up! We need our drinks!"

A cosmic dance of leaves and stems,
In funny hats, they play like gems.
A succulent quips, "I'm quite aware,
You're looking at the greenest affair!"

So here they jive, all together,
Amidst the glass, they plot forever.
With giggles sprouting through the fog,
Living the dreams of a garden blog!

Glass Gardens in a Bottle

Bottled worlds with lidded tops,
Where daisies dance and clover hops.
Inside, the tiny creatures squeal,
As time stands still, a fun surreal.

"Hey, ants! Bring sugar, make it sweet!"
"Don't forget the crumbs for a treat!"
The ladybugs plan a fancy feast,
While gnats are voted the annoying beast.

Peeking through the glassy dome,
A playground that feels like home.
Every inch a joy to roam,
In bustling joys, we all can comb.

So take a look and laugh aloud,
At tiny fun, both weird and proud.
In this little sanctuary,
Laughter thrives, it's quite the spree!

Whispers of the Miniature World

In a jar, there's mischief bound,
Where little worlds spin round and round.
"Did you hear?" the sprout began,
"There's a gnome who dances—yeah, the man!"

A spider swings from leaf to leaf,
While snails debate if they're too brief.
Funny tales of garden lore,
An ivy laughs and starts to snore.

"Let's throw a party! Gather near!"
The petals chirp, the mosses cheer.
A glimmering glass, all aglow,
As nature's quirks begin to flow.

So lift your gaze and join the fun,
In this jar, all life is one.
With whispers soft and laughter loud,
Become a part of the tiny crowd!

Slivers of Earth Encased

In a jar, I found a world,
Where tiny creatures dance and twirl.
Moss wears a crown, and ferns take a bow,
Who knew plants could party? Oh, wow!

Life's a circus beneath the lid,
With bugs and soil, their antics slid.
When I peek in, it's hard to miss,
That lettuce laughs when you give a kiss!

Stuck in glass, they smile and sway,
What secrets lie they cannot say.
I tell them jokes, they giggle back,
In this odd space, no humor lacks!

Each tiny root has a story bright,
Of sunlit days and starry night.
Oh, if only we could join their glee,
In this green kingdom, just them and me!

Holding onto Leafy Dreams

In dreamlike shades of green and gold,
A leafy realm, away from the cold.
Laughter bubbles from dirt's embrace,
A funny fruit with a silly face.

Little sprouts in a glassy dome,
Count their blessings, feel right at home.
If plants could speak, they'd share a riddle,
And make us giggle from dawn till middle.

The soil whispers secrets of the day,
As branches dance in a quirky sway.
'Why did the flower cross the road?'
To get to the sun, in its abode!

So here we ponder, in their greenspace,
With silly smiles, they claim their place.
For in this world, all's mischief and mirth,
Just leafing through, finding our worth!

Captured Harmony Beneath Glass

A glassy bubble, a leafy spree,
All my worries now seem so free.
Each sprig and stalk, a chuckle bright,
Holding hands in the morning light.

The tiny pond in a jar does cheer,
With fish that giggle, let's all hear!
When I tap the glass, they all play shy,
But peek-a-boo makes time flutter by!

Caught in a dance, the roots entwine,
While sprouting stories of the divine.
"I'm a cactus, I've got sharp wit,"
"Don't poke fun or you might just split!"

Under glass, it's a whimsical show,
With flowers wearing hats, don't you know?
In this quirky box, life's always merry,
Where nature's joke is never contrary!

Oases of Time in Fragile Domes

In a fragile dome, the clock does pause,
While leaves engage in comic brawls.
Every petal boasts a favorite tattle,
As critters spin tales, a lively battle!

Who knew that ferns could crack a grin,
As earthworms join in, and say, "Let's begin!"
With roots below plotting their schemes,
In these little worlds, we find our dreams.

Each drop of dew, a pearl so bright,
Reflecting laughs in the soft moonlight.
A tiny snail dances, slow but spry,
Exclaiming, "Life's zooming, oh my, oh my!"

In this lush home, time's a fun mime,
With punchlines sprouting, it's always prime.
So come join the chaos, this leafy delight,
In fragile oases, where hearts feel light!

Enigma of the Living Glass

In jars of green, where secrets roam,
Tiny worlds thrive, yet feel like home.
A frog in one, with dreams to fly,
Cracks jokes with snails, oh me, oh my!

Sunlight giggles, with shadows that dance,
Cacti waltz, given half a chance.
When water's poured, a splashy parade,
As algae giggle in their green brigade.

Here's a moss that wears a tiny hat,
Talking to pebbles about where they're at.
A leaf whispers secrets, bold and spry,
In this quirky realm, it's fly or die!

So raise a glass to the lives unseen,
In this leafy circus, where all's routine.
With a wink and a twist, they plot and scheme,
In their whimsical world, they're living the dream!

Cycle of Enclosed Life

In miniature lands, with laughter and grins,
Beetles do stunts, and the party begins.
A squirrel once claimed, it's a nutty place,
As roots stretch forth, with a daring face.

Round and round, like a merry-go-round,
Time spins swiftly, without a sound.
A worm in a tie gives the plants a wink,
While a spider weaves webs for gossip to link.

The bugs hold a meeting, all tapping their feet,
Exchanging wild rumors over a treat.
With petals so bright, they dance in a queue,
In a circular rhythm, quite merry and new.

So here's to the cycles that never stop,
In glassy confines, where laughter won't drop.
With critters and plants, this joy never fades,
As we witness the antics of leafy charades!

Fractal Time in Greenery

In layers of green, the minutes unfold,
Each leaf a story, quirky and bold.
A beetle counts seconds with quirky haste,
While ferns reminisce of a past they embraced.

The moss hums a tune, a cheeky refrain,
Tickling the roots like a playful rain.
A turtle on a mission, moves in slow motion,
As time does a jig, in this glassy ocean.

Frogs conduct symphonies in frothy delight,
While daisies club, under radiant light.
The minutes stretch out, like vines that entwine,
In fractals of mirth, where the silly shines.

So let's toast to nature, in playful array,
With laughter and greenery leading the way.
As time gently chuckles, in giggles and rhymes,
In this funky kingdom, forever it climbs!

Petals of the Past

In glassy pockets, where memories dwell,
Petals recount tales, they giggle and tell.
A flower complains about days gone by,
While a sprout winks, as if to imply.

"Oh remember," it starts, "when we were so small?
A bug pulled a prank, and we laughed through it all!"
Dandelions puff, like little balloons,
Sharing wild tales 'neath the light of the moons.

In cozy confines, where time is a jest,
The leaves toss their heads, fully dressed in their best.
"Was that one a bouquet or simply a sneeze?
We'll never know, just say 'bless you' with ease!"

So here's to the petals, bright and absurd,
Caught in a dance, with the quirkiest word.
In fragments of moments, they playfully cling,
As echoes of laughter through foliage ring!

A Still Canvas of Nature

In glassy domes, the plants do grin,
With silly faces, they spin and spin.
They whisper secrets, laugh and play,
While we just watch, what a funny ballet!

The soil quakes with giggles here,
As roots tickle each other, oh dear!
A cactus wearing a tiny hat,
Sips tea with a snail, imagine that!

The sun shines bright, a spotlight's beam,
On vibrant green - a florist's dream.
A fern cracks jokes with a sprightly pet,
In this small world, there's laughter yet!

Each drop of dew, a glistening cheer,
In nature's stage, where nothing's queer.
They plot and plan with glee galore,
In a still canvas - who could ask for more?

Little Worlds

In glassy globes, the small things play,
Dancing around, in their own ballet.
A mushroom twirls, a mossy waltz,
And critters greet with no adult faults.

Spiders in tuxedos spin webs anew,
While ladybugs wear red with a view.
The ants are chefs, cooking up a feast,
With crumbs as treats, they never cease!

A pebble philosopher sips morning dew,
Cracking jokes that only plants knew.
Here, violets joke with a pinkish hue,
Each day an episode, laughable too!

Beneath the glass, they build their dreams,
In tiny realms, bursting at the seams.
With a giggle and wink, they flaunt their glee,
Oh, what a sight, this giddy spree!

Lengthened Moments

Inside a jar, where shadows loom,
The little critters break the gloom.
A dragonfly juggles with flair,
While butterflies dance without a care.

Snails with swagger glide with grace,
Moving slowly in this quirky space.
The days stretch long, laughter fills the air,
As plants throw parties without a spare!

A crooked smile from a wayward vine,
Makes you chuckle, oh how divine!
They stretch and reach for the moonlit glow,
With antics that steal the starry show!

In the quiet hum of this whimsical space,
Nature's comedians embrace their place.
As time twists softly, they sway in rhyme,
Creating moments that tickle the prime!

Timeless Tenderness in a Miniature Realm

In a bottle of joy, the greens grow bright,
Sharing whispers in the soft twilight.
A tiny tree swings with a cheeky grin,
While a wise old stone looks on with a chin.

The bubbles blow laughter, bursting free,
As worms collaborate in perfect spree.
With beetles in bowties doing their best,
Who knew such characters liked to jest?

A stretchy flower gives a yawn,
While crickets serenade the dawn.
Each tick of the clock, a giggle unplanned,
In this tender space where fun is unbanned!

Time is a jester in this lush retreat,
With minuscule worlds, oh so sweet.
The glass holds treasures, silly and grand,
Forever tickling dreams, unplanned!

Botanical Chronicles Behind Haze

Through foggy glass, the saga unfolds,
Of botanicals bold, with stories told.
A fern with flair tells tales of yore,
While thyme rolls dice for fun galore!

Mossy mats act as soft beds,
For gnomes who party and hang their heads.
Petals play dress-up, all in a row,
As sunlight peeks in, putting on a show!

A rogue little leaf spins wild and free,
Tickling the roots, promising glee.
With whispers of laughter from bumblebee queens,
This charming place fuels wondrous dreams!

Giddy plants dance with fervent delight,
In a bazaar of humor, what a sight!
Behind the haze, their antics don't cease,
In cozy chapters, we find sweet peace!

Timeless Soil

In a pot where the weeds play hide and seek,
The roots throw parties, it's quite unique.
Dirt on my shoes, but I don't really care,
I dance with the daisies, with laughter to share.

A worm just wiggled and offered a drink,
Sipping on rainwater, we just can't think.
The sun is the DJ, spinning good vibes,
While the ants are the bouncers, guarding their tribes.

Life in a Petite Universe

Tiny worlds thrive in glassy havens,
Where bamboo and ferns throw leafy raves in.
The moss is a carpet, plush and inviting,
While the snails discuss dreams, quite exciting!

A ladybug strutting in polka-dot flair,
While the spiders are judging the guests with a stare.
The clouds are just fluff on the ceiling above,
Offering shade to the creatures in love.

Secrets Beneath the Surface

Beneath the green skin, there's chatter galore,
With roots telling tales of adventures in store.
A gnome sits on guard, with a grin on his face,
While the earthworms conspire to win the race.

A pebble's a gem with aspirations grand,
Whispers of treasures, oh isn't it grand?
The soil keeps secrets that tickle the ground,
While mushrooms join in with their whimsical sound.

The Clockwork of Leaves

Clock hands made of ivy tick-tock away,
Each leaf is a moment in green shades of play.
The branches stretch out, waving to the breeze,
While the sun's beams tickle the rustling leaves.

With acorns as currencies, we trade for delight,
And squirrels plan parties that go through the night.
In this little world where the quirky things bloom,
Time dances in circles, while flowers consume.

The Beauty of Moments Past

In glassy worlds where laughter reigns,
Little plants dance, forgetting pains.
Tiny figures play hide and seek,
While roots gossip, oh so unique.

Memories trapped in layers of green,
A time machine, if you know what I mean!
Watch the ferns shake their leafy heads,
As if to say, 'Where are our beds?'

Each bauble holds a fleeting cheer,
As crickets chirp, ever so near.
We crack a joke, they mimic our tone,
In this vivid realm, we're never alone.

So sprinkle fun in every sphere,
Life's fleeting moments, bring them near.
In these capsules, the past's a hoot,
With laughter sprouting, oh how cute!

Life Paused in Crystal

Glass prisons filled with green delight,
Hiding secrets, both day and night.
Watch as the mosses wiggle and play,
Time never wears them down, no way.

A sprinkle of water, a wink from a bug,
Caught in a dance, who gives a shrug?
The soil whispers tales of long-gone days,
As we peer in, amazed in a daze.

Sunbeams tickle leaves with so much glee,
While beetles pretend to be high and free.
In this little world where nothing's a crime,
Every second stretches, just like time.

So take a peek and share a grin,
Life is a laugh, let the fun begin.
With a smirk and a wink, the stories unfold,
In crystal chambers, the past is retold.

Green Timelines in Capsule Form

Cacti stand tall like old-time pros,
In their tiny kingdom, anything goes.
They chuckle softly, 'Remember that part?'
As we lean closer, gazing heart to heart.

Mossy layers tell of days gone by,
While ladybugs race as if to fly.
Each bubble holds a moment so sweet,
In this pocket of green, we can't be beat.

Time ticks softly, like a muted drum,
As beetles debate on where they come from.
With a smile, they nod, 'We're here for the show!'
Life's a punchline, and we're all in the know!

So find a jar, let the fun begin,
Capture a giggle, collect the grin.
In leafy realms where memories vow,
Laughing with critters, life's a fun wow!

Nourishment for Hours Within

In a jar where the laughter brews,
The tiniest sprouts share the good news.
Watch them munch on sunlight and cheer,
As we peek inside, our worries disappear.

Crickets serenade the curious ants,
Who waltz with the sprouts, in funny pants.
Each flicker of leaves, a moment's tease,
In this little world, nothing's too serious, please!

Sipping on sunshine, they giggle and sway,
Telling stories of adventures 'day by day.
Each leaf a canvas, a story untold,
In this glassy realm, life shines like gold.

So join the party, don't be shy,
Echoes of laughter will surely fly.
In this vast expanse of green delight,
Nourishment flows, oh, what a sight!

Enchanted Capsules of Flora

In glassy homes, the plants all giggle,
With tiny frogs that start to wriggle.
A spider spins with silken flair,
While snails slow dance without a care.

Mossy carpets fluff and sway,
As beetles roam in their ballet.
Each leaf a hat, each root a shoe,
In this small world, they play peekaboo!

Raining pebbles on a sunny day,
The sun's a lamp, the sky's a play.
A snail grins wide, a cactus waves,
We've found the place where joy behaves.

Here, reality's just a twist away,
With every turn, a new cliché.
We laugh at roots with curly hair,
And blossoms clad in berry wear.

Timeless Blooms in a Secluded Sphere

In a bubble of joy, the petals twirl,
Dancing flowers give the air a whirl.
A shy little bud takes a deep breath,
Wishing to dodge the hole of death.

Mossy hats on toadstool heads,
Giggles echo when a vine spreads.
A beetle's mustache twirls with pride,
As whispers float with each tiny stride.

The clock ticks slow for the lush array,
While roots tell tales in their own way.
A sunbeam peeks, making shadows play,
In this realm where moments drift and sway.

Each petal's laugh, a secret spell,
They charm the dust and cast it well.
When evening comes, they sleep and dream,
Of proud displays, a merry scheme.

The Dance of Shadows and Light

Under a dome where secrets peek,
The light has come to play hide and seek.
Leaves waltz around as shadows chase,
With laughter echoing all over the place.

A glimmer here, a shimmer there,
The guardian moss gives a cheeky stare.
Each pulse of color, a cheeky wink,
In a delicate world that loves to blink.

When dusk descends, the party's on,
The fireflies march till the break of dawn.
Tiny whispers fill the airy scene,
As spirits play like they're on a screen.

Twisted roots shape a funky groove,
In this dance where shadows prove.
When joy tilts the very ground,
A vibrant beat is what we've found.

Little Ecosystems, Big Stories

In tiny worlds, the dramas bloom,
Each day unfolds like a flower's plume.
Ants plot journeys on a leafy road,
While fairies giggle at the picnic load.

The lizards wear their hats askew,
As minuscule critters join the queue.
A whispering seed has tales to weave,
Of daring escapes that make you believe.

A squirrel hops, looking for a snack,
While chubby worms plot their next attack.
On this patch of earth, fables thrive,
Each drop of dew tells stories alive.

With every leaf, a legend unfurls,
In a realm where even dust swirls.
Who knew such fun could fit so tight,
In these little stories, oh what a sight!

Moments Caught in a Flora Waltz

In a jar, a little green,
A dancing fern, a sight unseen.
Bouncing bugs in tiny shoes,
Shuffling leaves, spreading the news.

Marbles rolling beneath the moss,
A snail cruising, oh, what a boss!
Worms breakdancing in the dirt,
While oh-so-chill vines just flirt.

Crickets chirp a funny tune,
Plant pals grooving 'neath the moon.
Succulents wearing sunglasses bright,
All in step, it feels just right.

With laughter locked in glassy walls,
Nature's party, how it enthralls!
Breathe it in, the silliness thrives,
In this world where joy arrives.

Reflections of Growth in Encased Moments

A cactus blooms, wears a shy grin,
While a hipster plant sips its gin.
Moss beards hang like an old chap,
As lizards join for a quick nap.

Fungi shout, "We're part of the crew!"
Their fluffy hats, a colorful view.
And the orbs of glass start to sway,
Imprisoned laughter keeps gloom at bay.

Jars of growth, with secrets to tell,
Each sprout a legend, oh so swell.
A cricket dons a bowtie so fine,
As roots do the cha-cha with vine.

With each poke and prod, they extend,
Fun finds a way to bend and blend.
In mirrored worlds, echoes of cheer,
Grow with giggles, that's why we're here.

Seasons Sealed Beneath the Surface

Winter's chill in a jar so neat,
Snowflakes swirl, it's a frosty treat.
A pine tree wears a winter cap,
And bugs are hosting a Christmas rap.

Spring hops in with a croaky song,
Where the mushrooms sing all night long.
Bees in bowties buzzing with flair,
Sippin' nectar with style and care.

Summer lies in a bright array,
Worms in shades, come out to play.
Sunflowers striking a yoga pose,
While ladybugs strike silly foes.

The fall comes wrapped in leaves of gold,
With critters trading their stories told.
In each layer, laughter and cheer,
Seasons sealed, the fun's always near.

Nature's Symphony within the Boundaries

A symphony of giggles escapes,
Tiny creatures all wearing capes.
Frogs at the mic, ready to sing,
While earthworms rock out in a ring.

Grasshoppers write their own little score,
While moss takes a bow, wanting more.
Roots conduct the craziest bands,
Sharing a dance of wiggly hands.

With petals flapping in a grand tune,
Even the sunlight joins in soon.
Beetles jive under glowing beads,
Nature's chorus fulfills all needs.

Glass walls keep this laughter contained,
Where every crack holds joy unchained.
In boundless glee, life takes the stage,
Nature's antics, forever engage.

The Stillness of Nature's Clocks

In a jar of green, the moss does yawn,
As crickets chirp through early dawn.
The sun peeks in with a cheeky grin,
While sleepy plants plot their next spin.

A snail moves fast, oh what a race,
Yet takes an hour to change its place.
The stones whisper tales of days gone by,
In their quiet world, no need to fly.

Flowers flirt with specks of dust,
In this little world, who can we trust?
A cloud drifts by, but just for fun,
It stops to chat, then cuddles the sun.

So here's to worlds in glassy halls,
Where time is slow and laughter calls.
With nature's joy in sealed-up space,
Life's little quirks we all must embrace.

Verdant Sanctuaries

Leafy temples in glassy homes,
Where tiny beasts and moss can roam.
A gathering of greens, a feathery crew,
All waiting for cheese—their dreams come true!

With squeaky toys beneath the fronds,
The lizards lounge and create their bonds.
A dancing beetle draws a crowd,
While shy ferns blush beneath a shroud.

A clever worm claims he's a star,
While hiding from a watchful jar.
The sunlight glints on snails in suits,
Their tiny parties with roots for boots!

So let's toast to our tiny abodes,
Where laughter mingles with gentle codes.
In these green havens, we shall reside,
Finding joy with each little slide.

Crystals of the Past

A gleaming shard sits all alone,
With tales of oceans, it claims its throne.
It thinks it's fancy, a stuck-up gem,
But really, it just wants to meet a hem.

Stuck in the past, these rocks can brag,
About the time they were a mud flag.
A pebble chuckles, 'I'm the real prize!'
'At least I don't glisten with antique lies.'

The sands of yore give a snicker or two,
As they argue over who's more blue.
But every glimmer comes with a fight,
Will they sparkle, or wilt in the light?

These treasures speak of dreams gone awry,
Shining brightly, but oh, they sigh.
In their crystal thoughts, they'make us smile,
With secrets hidden, all the while.

Fragments of a Secluded Cosmos

In jars of stars, the view is grand,
Where comets gossip and meteors stand.
A tiny thing trembles in space so bold,
Dreaming of kingdoms made of gold.

Each fragment you see has a tale to spin,
Of galactic raves where the fun begins.
They bounce off walls with shimmering flair,
While aliens peek with a curious stare.

A nebula whispers, 'Why so serious?'
While dancing in circles, looking delirious.
The planets spin in a cosmic game,
Daring each other to win the fame.

So let's hold tight to our little sphere,
With laughter and joy that's sincere.
In this secluded dome, let's find delight,
As the universe giggles throughout the night.

Echoes of Green Beneath Glass

In a jar where critters play,
Mighty moss holds stories at bay.
A snail in a race, oh what a sight,
Sipping on shadows, embracing the night.

Bugs have meetings under glass roofs,
Discussing life in tiny goofs.
The ferns conspire, whisper and tease,
While the stems sway gently in the breeze.

Laughter echoes in layers of soil,
As roots twist around, making a coil.
Every leaf has a tale to unfold,
In the secret world, bright and bold.

A cactus grins, with spines so sharp,
While a sleepy fern strums a harp.
Who knew plants could giggle and dance?
In glassy homes, they take every chance.

Dust and Dew in the Glasshouse

Inside the glass, droplets play,
Like tiny fairies at dawn's first ray.
Sweet sunlight splashes on leaves so bright,
As dust bunnies dance in pure delight.

The pots have tales of wild, wild dreams,
While succulents stretch and plot their schemes.
Who knew a fern could tell a joke,
With leaves that wiggle and gently poke?

Creeping vines have a secret game,
Entwining friends, never the same.
A glasshouse party, all are in tow,
With laughter sprouting, stealing the show.

But watch your step on that dusty floor,
You might just trip on a rubber plant's lore.
In this quirky kingdom, who needs a sign?
For every leaf here knows how to shine.

Still Life in a Living Frame

A portrait of green in a wooden frame,
Where succulents whisper and play the game.
Each petal smiles, some blush with glee,
While the orchids plot, 'What next shall be?'

Stillness reigns, or so they say,
But watch those ferns — they're plotting away!
A beetle prances from leaf to leaf,
In this artwork of chaos, joy, and belief.

Moss sprawls like an artist's brush,
Colorful stories come alive in a hush.
When dusk falls, they whisper and scheme,
Creating reflections straight from a dream.

In this frame full of whimsy and cheer,
A world appears, both far and near.
They giggle at time, for who needs a clock?
These playful plants are the real talk.

Seeds of Serenity Encased

Within the glass, adventures lie,
With seeds that giggle and dreams that fly.
A sunflower dances with an elegant sway,
While tiny sprouts plan a bold cabaret.

Each droplet of dew, a sparkling spy,
Observing life, beneath the sky.
In a world encased, time takes a nap,
While the cacti argue who's the best chap.

Beneath the earth, a party awaits,
Where roots take orders, debating the traits.
A worm rides in, making quite the scene,
In this vibrant kingdom, everything's keen.

So here we chuckle, at green shenanigans,
With every leaf, a ripple of plans.
In these bizarre realms, laughter rings true,
As nature's comedy show swings into view.

www.ingramcontent.com/pod-product-compliance
Lightning Source LLC
Chambersburg PA
CBHW070322120526
44590CB00017B/2783